WITHDRAWN

Gumdrop 15.95

Monkeys

Baby Animals

ALICE TWINE

PowerKids press
New York

HUNTINGTON CITY-TOWNSHIP
PUBLIC LIBRARY
200 W. Market Street
Huntington IN 46750

Published in 2008 by The Rosen Publishing Group, Inc.
29 East 21st Street, New York, NY 10010

Copyright © 2008 by The Rosen Publishing Group, Inc.

All rights reserved. No part of this book may be reproduced in any form without permission in writing from the publisher, except by a reviewer.

First Edition

Editor: Amelie von Zumbusch
Book Design: Julio Gil
Photo Researcher: Nicole Pristash

Photo Credits: Cover, p. 1 © Anup Shah/Getty Images; pp. 5, 7, 9, 11, 13, 15, 17, 19, 21, 23, 24 (top left, top right, bottom left, bottom right) © Shutterstock.com.

Library of Congress Cataloging-in-Publication Data

Twine, Alice.
  Monkeys / Alice Twine. — 1st ed.
      p. cm.
  Includes index.
  ISBN-13: 978-1-4042-3775-9 (library binding)
  ISBN-10: 1-4042-3775-5 (library binding)
  1. Monkeys—Infancy—Juvenile literature. I. Title.
  QL737.P93T85 2008
  599.8—dc22
                                              2006100462

Manufactured in the United States of America.

Contents

Baby Monkeys — 4

Kinds of Baby Monkeys — 8

A Baby Monkey's Life — 16

Words to Know — 24

Index — 24

Web Sites — 24

Monkey mothers take good care of their babies.

Monkey babies are good at using their hands. Monkeys have five fingers, just as people do. They even have **fingernails**!

There are hundreds of different kinds of monkeys. This baby monkey is a squirrel monkey.

These monkeys are baboons. Baboons live in big groups, called **troops**.

Big monkeys, like this young gorilla, are called apes. Gorillas are the largest kind of ape.

This young ape is a chimpanzee. Chimpanzees live in Africa. They are very smart.

Monkey babies, like this squirrel monkey, often ride around on their mother's back.

This mother gorilla is **grooming** her baby. Grooming keeps monkeys clean.

When they are very young, monkeys drink their mother's milk. As they grow older, monkeys eat many foods, such as nuts, seeds, and **fruit**.

This young gorilla is having fun swinging on a rope. Young monkeys like to play, just like children do.

Words to Know

fingernail

fruit

grooming

troop

Index

B
baboons, 10

F
fingernails, 6

fruit, 20

G
gorilla(s), 12, 18, 22

Web Sites

Due to the changing nature of Internet links, PowerKids Press has developed an online list of Web sites related to the subject of this book. This site is updated regularly. Please use this link to access the list:
www.powerkidslinks.com/baby/monkeys/